Contents

INTRODUCTION

Hello and thank you for purchasing this book. I am super excited that you have decided to begin this process of healing from toxic relationships and have a desire to create healthy relationships.

Beware, this book can change the way you see yourself and your future connections to others. I do not claim to be a relationship expert. However, I am a trained expert at recognizing toxic relationships, understanding their impact and creating healthy boundaries. This book was born out of my personal and professional experiences - seeing many women experience toxic relationships, often asking why, yet repeating the same patterns.

As a child, I did not see many marital relationships, nor was I exposed to consistent, loving and healthy relationships between a man and a woman on any level. As a young adult, I constantly had the sense that I was learning as I went. I was a good student. Every situation was new. I experienced quite a few toxic relationships, but I say with pride that I never experienced the same type of toxic relationship twice.

I have experienced the liar, the cheater, the thief, the almost abusive and possessive, the alcoholic, the lazy and the unemployed. Even as a young adult, I studied behaviors, I studied what was good and what was not good for me. I became unapologetic about what I was not going to tolerate and yet I still found myself in unhealthy relationships. I loved hard and I loved freely, and I believed unconsciously that love would be enough, that love would be what was necessary to make any relationship work... I was wrong.

Becoming a mental health therapist however brought a heightened level of awareness of how toxic relationships impact not only the woman involved, but also her family unit. It was through my practice of therapy and consistent study, that I discovered just how many women experience unhealthy relationships and the long-lasting effects. I found that as wonderful as these women were, they each experienced a consistent pattern, getting hurt again and again from toxic relationships. Even though many of them were exposed to committed relationships growing up, they still found themselves in toxic situations. I combined my knowledge and experience to develop formal steps to assist women through the process of healing from toxic relationships and developing a system for the art of dating healthy.

This book was written to help women who find themselves in unhealthy relationship after unhealthy relationship and want to end the cycle. For women who desire to love themselves so much that they are willing to do the work to truly heal. For women who unapologetically want to be free to love without the fear of being hurt again. And finally, this book is for women who want to avoid the toxicity that comes with toxic relationships.

And so, I studied and implemented, woman after woman who came into my office with signs of depression, anxiety, low self-esteem, a feeling of stuck and/or defeated. Week after week, step after step many of the ladies unknowingly were undergoing what is now the, "Heal, Date, Thrive" process. Utilizing the process, I have seen results and so did they. Women begin to truly heal from toxic relationships and create healthy dating boundaries in order to truly thrive.

This book can help you heal and assist you in creating your individualized plan for healthy relationships. While this book is intended to be an individual guide, it is also recommended to use the stages within one of the, "Heal, Date, Thrive," platforms, (Private Facebook group, HDT Woman's Circle, or one-on-one Intensive Healing Coaching), or with a licensed mental health therapist. The benefits of including a professional outside source is that you receive a non-judgmental perspective from someone who will guide you to truly look at yourself. They will also motivate you to stick with it, help you identify and correct any faulty thoughts that hold you back from your true healing. The methods in this book are tried-and-true and will work together to help you genuinely Heal, Date and Thrive.

WHAT IS IT?

What is it that can make a woman have sleepless nights?

That can make the healthiest woman lose her appetite?

What is it that can cause a professional woman to lose her focus and concentration?

That can make the most beautiful woman question her value and worth?

What is it that can cause the most intelligent woman to do unintelligent things for unintelligent people?

That can make the happiest woman cry until there are seemingly no tears left?

What is it that can make a woman feel so loved one minute and unloved the next?

What can cause excitement and hope one day but confusion and rejection the very next day?

Have you figured it out yet?

That thing is the, "wrong male."

When you experience the, “wrong male,” you are often left with two questions:

1. Why did this happen to me?
2. How do I get past it?

THE WHY

As a therapist, friend, sister, daughter, but most importantly as a woman, I have found that there is one primary reason why women experience the wrong male.You see this thing called the, "wrong Male," has nothing to do with your appearance, race, income, educational level, career status, church status, how many children you have or don't have, age, nor your ethnicity. The, wrong male, experience is simply a woman thing.

Women all around the world experience the, "wrong male," you are not alone. While there is something to say about women who grew up without a father, those who grew up with a father in the home, but was a poor example, women who didn't experience love and affection growing up and to those who were abused and/or molested. I can also tell you, through my studies and research, years of conversations and simply living, I have found that women who grew up with a father, even a good example of a father will experience the, wrong male." Those who were never molested or abused have experienced the wrong male. Those who grew up with love and affection every day of their life will at some point, experience the wrong male.

I can go through reasons why women want to believe a man, why you want to be loved, why you want to give your all into that dream. I can certainly go through reasons why he behaves the way he does. They can stem from having to do with a lack of love or lack of discipline or simply wanting to take the easy way out. I can hypothesize that he simply is not strong or courageous enough to do things the right way. I could go on and on about how cowardly the he is or how insecure he must be or focus on his inability to effectively communicate. I could discuss how he was raised in a society that teaches and condones his behaviors. I could go on and on about reasons why we as women experience him or why he was taught to be this way, but I much rather focus on our healing and getting unstuck.

"We often get trapped in trying to figure out "the why's," that we forget to seek healing."

This book is designed to help you heal through past hurt, take a deeper look at yourself and what you truly want in a relationship. By the end of this book, you will have developed your individualized plan for your healthy dating.

THE HOW

After experiencing him, we are often left with the questions of how do we get past the hurt, pain, betrayal of trust, and the decrease in self-confidence? Three truths you must understand and commit to:

1. Understand that getting past it is absolutely possible.
2. Recognize that healing is a process - it will take time and work.
3. The process works - trust the process and do the work.

Now that you understand these three truths, let's explore how this process works.

There are three primary steps are: healing, dating and thriving. It is recommended that you go through each process alone. If you are just beginning to heal, you should also not date or you should not enter the thriving process while learning to date.

As you go through each process, take the time to truly explore each area. While it is often the automatic response to read through the book and quickly jot things down, understand that your healing will come by way of time and true progression. So, after you read through the entire book, (if that's what you decide), go back and explore each step in more detail. For each step take a minimum of three days to truly think about and answer each question. If you get to a question that you are stuck on, ask others what they see/saw, (be mindful to take it as a learning process and not an attack).

"It was a process to get hurt, it will take a process to heal."

Each step in the process is one that is designed for you to gain insight into who you are, your experiences thus far and where you ultimately want to be. At the end of each step, there are affirmations you should recite or space to list yours. An affirmation is a positive assertion/declaration you make about yourself. They are statements you say to yourself that are true, but often not believed, the goal is that you say the affirmation until it becomes fact for you.

This is often harder than one may think,but it gets easier with practice. With each affirmation, go to the mirror and look yourself in the eyes and speak it. Every time you see a mirror, speak it. Speak it until you truly believe it. Speak it until you are healed.

Now that you have a clear understanding of WHY the "Wrong Male" experience happens and have the guidelines for how you will get past it...

Let's get to work!

Process 1
Heal.

HEAL

How to heal from your experience with the,
"Wrong Male."

As you explore this chapter, think about your current, most recent, or most damaging experience with the wrong male. The next six steps will guide you through the process of healing from the pain you endured. Healing is a process so don't rush through the steps. Take your time and be intentional about the true purpose - healing.

"Healing is a process that takes time, but you are worth the time and work to be completely healed."

Affirmation: "Healing is a process and I will heal."

Recite this affirmation daily or create your own affirmation about this new healing process, write it down:

____

____

____

1. FORGIVENESS

Before you can truly heal, you must first forgive yourself for choosing him or allowing yourself to be chosen. While your hurt and frustration exists, it may be hard to understand how and why you ever held a conversation with him. Why you didn't walk away sooner? Part of the self forgiveness process is recognizing that you liked and saw something positive in him, no matter how small or large. Think back to when you first met, when things were good or when you needed something. It is important to recognize that there were reasons why you loved him.

He offered something that you liked. Become OK with whatever you discover and accept it. This step is important because you will see that you had good reason at the time for holding the conversation, for staying in the relationship, and for loving him.

"You are not stupid, crazy or any other term you may have given yourself You were blinded. But now, you begin to take the blinders off."

Now write it down. Write as much good as you can think of, no matter how big or small. Get detailed and give examples. Was it that dance, the way he made you feel, that time he had your back when no one else understood? Take your

time and add to your list over the next several days. Still can't remember the positives?
Take a look at the list of positive traits at the back of the book.

The "Wrong Male" that I dated had the following good qualities/traits:

1.______________________________

2.______________________________

3.______________________________

4.______________________________

5.______________________________

6.______________________________

7.______________________________

8.______________________________

9.______________________________

10.______________________________

11.______________________________

12.______________________________

13.______________________________

14.______________________________

15.______________________________

Next, acknowledge there were some occasions that were fun and loving, these things made you want him even more. Describe those positive occasions and how he made you feel:

1.____

____

2.____

____

3.____

____

4.____

____

5.____

____

6.____

____

7.____

____

8.____

____

9.____

____

10.____

____

Affirmation: "I forgive myself for what I didn't see at the time. I will learn from it and become better because of it."

Recite this affirmation daily or create your own affirmation about forgiveness, write it below:

____

____

____

Here you can write additional reflections about the steps of forgiveness. Are there additional thoughts, ideas, or challenges you must correct? Write it here:

2. IDENTIFY YOUR VULNERABILITIES

Now that you have accepted there were reasons for loving the wrong male and have forgiven yourself, you must now identify vulnerabilities, weaknesses, and red flags that led to the unhealthy relationship.

"When someone shows you who they are, believe them. ~ Maya Angelou"

What is that thing that you want that makes you weak? Do you love a good-looking man, who is sexually satisfying, financially secure, and includes you in family events or talks about wanting a family with you? Maybe it is his strong religious beliefs? Someone that supports your dreams? Accepting of your perceived flaws that you don't think most would? What is that thing that causes your judgment to be swayed? He must have ______ to get you? It is important to be honest with yourself. If you are not aware of your vulnerabilities, weaknesses and desires, you will likely become weak again.

List your vulnerabilities, weaknesses and red flags:

1.____

2.____

3.____

4.____

5.____

6.____

7.____

8.____

9.____

10._______________________________________

Affirmation: "I will no longer allow my weaknesses to guide my actions, instead I will be purposeful about my choices."

Recite this affirmation daily or create your own affirmation about identifying your vulnerabilities, write it down and practice it daily:

____

____

____

Here you can write additional reflections about this step.

Are there additional thoughts, ideas, or challenges you must correct? Write it here:

3. LEARN THE LESSON

We must become ok with being wrong, and not getting it right the first, second, or tenth time. Understanding, you may have never read a dating guide (until now!). Yes, you may have read articles, watched shows about dating, but the reality is many women learn as we go. Some of us are slower learners, while others never took the time or didn't know how to figure out the lesson. It is now time to figure out the lesson.

Compare your two list on the previous pages and reflect on the lessons you learned. What was a turning point that you ignored at the time, why? What was the character trait you dismissed, why? What will you do different next time? In order to learn from your unhealthy relationship, you must gain a clear understanding of the lesson and learn from it. Write what you learned through your pain, what did you learn about yourself? What will you be sure to look out for next time?

1.____

____

2.____

____

3.____

____

4.____

____

5.____

____

6.____

____

7.____

____

Affirmation: "My past hurt is preparing me to avoid future hurt."

Recite this affirmation daily or create your own affirmation about your ability to learn from past hurt:

____

____

____

Write additional reflections about this step below. Are there additional thoughts, ideas, or challenges you must correct? Write it here:

4. EVIDENCE OF RESILIENCE

Your experience nor circumstance defines you. This pain experience, and current state are only temporary. You will get through it and you will be better in the end.

Look at your past, recognize all the trials, hard times and experiences with pain that you came out of. Know this is temporary and preparing you for the next healthy relationship.

"Healing is a process and does not happen overnight, rust the process, put in the work, your healing is around the corner."

List some trials you have made it through, explore those days when you didn't think you could take anymore. Remind yourself of your resilience.

"I know I can get through ______________________ since I made it through..."

List some situations you made it through, no matter how big or small, no matter how long ago. Recognize that as you have made it in the past, you will make it out of this.

Healing Is Power!

1. ______________________________

2. ______________________________

3. ______________________________

4. ______________________________

5. ______________________________

6. ______________________________

7. ______________________________

8. ______________________________

9. ______________________________

10. ______________________________

Affirmations: "This pain is temporary, I am an overcomer." Recite this affirmation daily or create your own affirmation about your evidence of resilience.

____

____

____

Write additional reflections about this step below. Are there additional thoughts, ideas, and challenges you need to correct? Write it here:

5. REMEMBER YOUR GREATNESS

You must remind yourself who you are and whose you are. Who were you before you met him? Who are you now? What are your talents and gifts? What is your potential? What will you become? It is important to remember that you are more than your current situation. If you are a believer, remember what God says about you, what are the promises for your life?

Once you can truly see your greatness, your healing becomes inevitable. If you need assistance, take a look at the positive traits list at the back of this book for assistance. List your positive traits here:

1.____

2.____

3.____

4.____

5.____

6.____

7.____

8.____

9.____

10.____

11.____

12.____

13.____

14.____

15.____

Affirmation: "I am smart, beautiful and wonderfully made."

Recite this affirmation daily or create your own affirmation about your greatness.

____

____

____

List additional reflections about this step. Are there additional thoughts, ideas, and challenges you need to correct? Write it here:

6. WORKING THROUGH THE PAIN

Until this point, I have given you affirmations to state. It is now time for you to create your own affirmations that speak to who you are right now. You must remind yourself daily, several times a day of your true worth. Every time you look in the mirror, recite your affirmations.

Decide on 2-3 affirmations, (recycle some of the affirmations you created in the previous steps or create new ones), that speak life to your situation. Affirmations should be spoken positively stating what you are or will be rather than what you are not or will stop doing.

Good examples of effective affirmations.

1. "I am smart, creative and an awesome catch."
2. "I am more than this temporary situation."
3. "I will be loved as I deserve to be loved!"

Examples of ineffective affirmations.

1. "I will stop crying and feeling sad." - What you focus on will stay in your mind. In this example, crying and feeling sad. It is very difficult to teach your mind not to do something negative however much easier to train your brain to think positive.

Consider instead –
"I will be happy today, I will smile and find things to laugh at."

2. "I won't make that mistake again." - In this example you unconsciously blame yourself which will only cause further negative feelings. Nor does this affirmation tell you what to do.

Consider instead –
"I have learned from my mistakes and I am now wiser."

3. "I can't allow myself to be mad." - Being mad is natural and can sometimes motivate you to change.However, if you hold on to the anger it can cause more damage for yourself, focus on what you do want.

Consider instead –
"I am happy, I woke up this day in my right mind, I am healing."

What affirmations will you commit to? Write them out, implement and adjust as necessary.

What are the affirmations you will recite every time you look in the mirror? Write them down and return weekly to add more affirmations.

1.____

____

2.____

____

3.____

____

4.____

____

5.____

____

6.____

____

7.____

____

8.____

____

9.____

____

10.____

____

Healing Is Power!

True change happens when you are consistent. Keeping track helps you to be consistent and actively maintain your healing!

"It is work.

You owe it to yourself to do the work."

When you said your affirmation, how did it feel?

Example:

04/11 - I said my affirmations most of the day. In the morning it felt weird, but I continued, and it did get easier. I am already beginning to believe this is temporary.

Keep up the good work. Continue to keep track of your affirmations. Date and describe how saying your affirmations are impacting you!

Additional options for working through the pain.

Find something to do that will keep you busy and remove the focus from what you are going through.

What are some hobbies you can do, tasks that require little to no mental thought, but can still provide a sense of accomplishment? What are some activities that have helped you get through difficult times in the past?
What are some tasks that you always wanted to do but never had the time?

Be intentional, list some possible hobbies, task, activities that you can use to occupy your thoughts:

____

____

____

____

____

____

____

____

____

____

If you could create the perfect place, real or imaginary, how would it look? How would it smell? How would you feel? Create that perfect place in your head then write it out. Once you have written it out, refocus your thoughts to that place whenever you get upset or begin to think negatively.

List additional reflections below. Are there additional thoughts, ideas, or challenges you must correct? Write it here:

Process 2
Date.

DATE.

Now that you have gone through the process of healing from your wrong male experience, it is now time to plan how you want to date going forward. The next four steps will cause you to explore your individual definition of what dating healthy means to you. Take your time, go through each step, put it down and then come back to it. Continue to add to your lists until you feel they are done.

BE INTENTIONAL

WHAT DO YOU WANT?

In order to date healthy and reach your relationship goals, you must first identify what your ideal relationship looks like. You will often find, what you seek to find.

"Without a plan, you will fall for anything."

What are your plans for love? What do you want? You must know what you want in order to recognize it when it comes. Do you want to date or get married? Do you want a monogamous or an open relationship? Do you want children or prefer no children? Without worrying about what your future mate would accept or what you think is available, in your heart, what do you want?

Understand that you were created for greatness and anything other than that is not for you. Don't settle for what is given to you, settle for what you need.

"Only settle for the best!"

What does the above statement mean to you? Everyone's best is different. This is not a question where you collaborate with your friends and family because everyone will have an opinion. Think about all the aspects of a relationship: income, appearance, family, social life, status, drinking, smoking, communication style, and personality.

What do you truly want?

Write your list. Get detailed. List no less than 10 wants - you are worth it.

Let's separate the needs from the wants.

Your wants are nice to have, but not necessary. Go back and place a star next to the non-negotiable items. As you date, refer to this list and become ok with not entertaining the guys who don't meet your needs.

"Become ok with hearing what he says and believe him."

Create your own affirmation about being intentional about what you want:

____

____

____

BE INTENTIONAL

AVOID THE TRAP

Many women find themselves in the obligation trap. They feel obligated to stay in unhealthy or nonproductive relationships due to a perceived/unhealthy belief or thought. In this instance, a woman will put up with things/situations they know they do not like or want in their life.

"Don't get caught in the obligation trap."

Examples:

- Dating the guy who can't find a job because you remember when you couldn't find a job.
- Kicking it with the guy who is selfish sexually because you remember when you couldn't satisfy an ex.
- Going out with the guy who smokes because you remember when you smoked or because you have friends and family that smoke.
- Dating the guy that drinks too much because you know someone who drinks way more, and they are fine.
- Entertaining the guy who doesn't have his own place because you know people who were in the same situation, they just needed a little bit of assistance.

- Spending time with the guy who has money, but does not take you anyplace. At least he comes to see you more than your previous man.
- Accommodating the guy who has a girlfriend and says he is "unhappy" because you remember being unhappy in your past relationship.

"Date based on who you are now not

who you used to be."

What are some traps you have experienced in your past? What have you convinced yourself to believe? In order to avoid making the same choices, you must be aware. Take some time to recognize traps that you could fall into if you are not careful. Be sure to date your responses.

Example: 12/03 "I have always wanted a family, if I am not careful, I will end up committing to the wrong guy again because he talks about wanting a family. Family men are a weakness for me. I have felt obligated to stay with someone because they promised me a family"

____

____

____

UNDERSTAND YOUR DEAL BREAKERS

What are your deal breakers? Go back to your red flags, vulnerabilities, and weaknesses. What things have you identified that should make you run in the other direction as soon as you see it? What are the things you know you cannot tolerate?

Lying? Cheating? Unemployed? Doesn't see his children? Bad hygiene? These are just examples. Some women are ok with someone who does not work because they like taking care of a man. There is no right or wrong, this is your plan. You must identify what will work for you.

What are your deal breakers? List them here. In some instances, write about why you chose them as a deal breaker. Truly understand what you don't want and why. The more understanding you have, the less likely you are to date someone with deal breakers.

While some may tell you, things are small or you should not worry about different deal breakers, become comfortable about what a deal breaker is for you. While too many deal breakers may cause you to be single for a longer period of time, you will also be without the pain, hurt, disappointment and frustration that comes from dating the wrong male. Stay connected to what you truly need in a relationship, be patient and intentional.

List your deal breakers:

1. ______________________________
2. ______________________________
3. ______________________________
4. ______________________________
5. ______________________________
6. ______________________________
7. ______________________________
8. ______________________________
9. ______________________________
10. ______________________________
11. ______________________________
12. ______________________________
13. ______________________________
14. ______________________________
15. ______________________________
16. ______________________________
17. ______________________________
18. ______________________________
19. ______________________________

YOUR RELATIONSHIP VALUE

You understand your value as an individual and all the strengths and positive traits you possess, but it is also important to understand your relationship value. When you begin to date, you should know and be able to communicate your value to your partner. This is important because as you recognize your relationship value you will look for your mate to bring relationship value as well. It is equally important that your future mate sees your values as important. If your relationship is gift giving, but your mate does not value that, will you end up not being yourself or feeling unappreciated?

"Your value is not tied to what you buy, but rather who you are."

What do you bring to a relationship? What do you offer?

Look at what you offer *now* not what you offered last year or 10 years ago. Do you communicate well? Are you supportive? What do you offer that sets you apart or makes you who you are? Understand your relationship value, write it out:

1. ______________________________

2. ______________________________

3. ______________________________

4. ______________________________

5. ______________________________

6. ______________________________

7. ______________________________

Another part of your relationship value is being aware of areas of your life you want to improve. What areas of your life are you working on developing? What are the areas you want to grow and what is your plan to accomplish it? In order to date healthy, you should be individually, physically, mentally and emotionally healthy. Having some focus on your own development, will keep you destined for continued greatness and less likely to attract and accept the wrong male.

"When you are unfulfilled you are more likely to seek the attention of the wrong male."

List areas of your life that you are interested in developing. Why is it important to you? What is your implementation plan?

1. ______________________________

2. ______________________________

3. ______________________________

Here you can write additional thoughts about areas of your life that you are interested in developing:

STICKING WITH IT

As you become intentional about dating healthy, it may seem difficult at times. During those times, ask yourself if this temporary difficulty is better than those sleepless nights, wet pillows from crying, anger and/or long-term consequences? The answer is yes. Your mental health is worth it.

Here is your benefit to writing during this process, review your notes and see what you have gone through. Identify your pros and cons and make an informed decision.

You got this!

Remind yourself why you are going through this process. Recall a painful experience. The time you felt stuck, the unmet expectation you never received. List just one or two here. The goal is to maintain your momentum. Your best life is not far away.

___

___

___

___

___

___

Process 3
Thrive!

THRIVE!

Congratulations! You have made it to phase three - Thrive! You have gone through the healing steps and have effective tools to avoid the pain endured by entertaining the wrong male. Let's activate what you know. Thrive. You can thrive when you know you are making decisions and steps that will help you excel in life and love. Here is when you begin that process of putting what you know to work.

"Even when we know what to do, we still choose wrong at times."

MINDFULNESS IN DATING

Now that you are clear about what you want in a relationship, what your deal breakers are and what your relationship value is, it is important to understand that those you allow in your circle, if only for a little while, can influence, disrupt, and affect your emotional well-being. I can't tell you how many times I have heard, "I didn't even like him like that or he was ugly, why do I care?" I've heard, "I knew he wasn't the one I just thought it would be fun to hang out with him. After all he was very funny, or he took me out a lot."

The reality is, the people you allow in your circle wear on you. You get comfortable. You tend to forget about those small flaws like he drinks too much, he is always busy, or he said he is not ready for a commitment. After all, you, "Don't even like him like that." The problem however is your feelings change, but his do not. Women often find themselves leading with their hearts because of course his, "non-verbal messages," say he feels the same as you do, but that does not mean he is drinking any less, going out less, or wants to settle down.

The wrong male can also have long term negative effects. Over time, he can become the abuser, child molester, drug addict and thief of your peace and joy. The wrong male can become your child's father, your source of shame and embarrassment, or your financial dependent. He can have long-term effects if you don't know what to look for and are not intentional about dating.

As you date, it is important to listen to what he says, but also watch his actions for consistency. I hate to say it, but those 90 days may be a great start! Write the messages he is telling you and compare them to his actions. Does he say he always has time for you, but then is unavailable when you call? Does he say he misses you one day, but can go days without calling? Does he tell you you're special, but hides you from family and friends? Does he say he is a believer, but never initiates church or prayer? Does he have a problem identifying you by name? Whatever it is... Listen and watch. Write it out! Keep track of all the special feelings but also pay attention when that voice says hmmm...

> *"When a man really wants to be with you long term, he will show you. He will make time for you. He will let you know with his words and actions."*

Your Dating Journal is designed to cause you to be intentional about dating. This is your place to list how you feel, (good and bad), at that time. Very often, we will feel one way, but forget about it when something goes well, or things get better. We dismiss the signs until we are emotionally connected and then it becomes too hard to walk away from the relationship. While it may be unrealistic to write every conversation down or every date, this Dating Journal is for you to write about days/incidents that stand out to you. Those times that you just don't feel comfortable or your gut is active, write it down. It does not mean things have to end there, it means that you are being intentional about what you want, understanding how you feel, learning about your own patterns and recognizing room for growth.

"If you are not mindful, the wrong male will make you believe it is all in your head."

As you journal, write without limit. Be free to feel what you feel. You are responsible for taking care of your emotional and mental health - do it.

Dating
Journal

DATING JOURNAL

Date:__________ Name of date:______________

Where were you?______________________________

What attracts you to him?

____

____

____

What stood out to you?

____

____

____

____

____

____

How did he make you feel?

____

____

____

Any red flags? YES or NO? If Yes, what was it?

____

____

____

____

____

____

DATING JOURNAL

Date:__________ Name of date:______________

Where were you?________________________________

What attracts you to him?

____

____

____

What stood out to you?

____

____

____

____

____

____

How did he make you feel?

____

____

____

Any red flags? YES or NO? If Yes, what was it?

____

____

____

____

____

____

DATING JOURNAL

Date:__________ Name of date:_______________

Where were you?_____________________________________

What attracts you to him?

____

____

____

What stood out to you?

____

____

____

____

____

____

How did he make you feel?

____

____

____

Any red flags? YES or NO? If Yes, what was it?

____

____

____

____

____

____

DATING JOURNAL

Date:__________ Name of date:______________

Where were you?______________________________

What attracts you to him?

What stood out to you?

How did he make you feel?

Any red flags? YES or NO? If Yes, what was it?

DATING JOURNAL

Date:__________ Name of date:_______________

Where were you?_________________________________

What attracts you to him?

____

____

____

What stood out to you?

____

____

____

____

____

____

How did he make you feel?

____

____

____

Any red flags? YES or NO? If Yes, what was it?

____

____

____

____

____

____

DATING JOURNAL

Date:__________ Name of date:_______________

Where were you?_______________________________________

What attracts you to him?

____

____

____

What stood out to you?

____

____

____

____

____

____

How did he make you feel?

____

____

____

Any red flags? YES or NO? If Yes, what was it?

____

____

____

____

____

____

DATING JOURNAL

Date:__________ Name of date:______________

Where were you?______________________________

What attracts you to him?

____
____
____

What stood out to you?

____
____
____
____
____
____

How did he make you feel?

____
____
____

Any red flags? YES or NO? If Yes, what was it?

____
____
____
____
____
____

DATING JOURNAL

Date:__________ Name of date:______________

Where were you?________________________________

What attracts you to him?

____

____

____

What stood out to you?

____

____

____

____

____

____

How did he make you feel?

____

____

____

Any red flags? YES or NO? If Yes, what was it?

____

____

____

____

____

____

DATING JOURNAL

Date:__________ Name of date:_______________

Where were you?_______________________________________

What attracts you to him?

____

____

____

What stood out to you?

____

____

____

____

____

____

How did he make you feel?

____

____

____

Any red flags? YES or NO? If Yes, what was it?

____

____

____

____

____

____

DATING JOURNAL

Date:__________ Name of date:_______________

Where were you?_____________________________________

What attracts you to him?

____

____

____

What stood out to you?

____

____

____

____

____

____

How did he make you feel?

____

____

____

Any red flags? YES or NO? If Yes, what was it?

____

____

____

____

____

____

DATING JOURNAL

Date:__________ Name of date:_______________

Where were you?____________________________________

What attracts you to him?

____

____

____

What stood out to you?

____

____

____

____

____

____

How did he make you feel?

____

____

____

Any red flags? YES or NO? If Yes, what was it?

____

____

____

____

____

____

DATING JOURNAL

Date:__________ Name of date:______________

Where were you?________________________________

What attracts you to him?

____

____

____

What stood out to you?

____

____

____

____

____

____

How did he make you feel?

____

____

____

Any red flags? YES or NO? If Yes, what was it?

____

____

____

____

____

____

DATING JOURNAL

Date:__________ Name of date:_______________

Where were you?____________________________________

What attracts you to him?

____

____

____

What stood out to you?

____

____

____

____

____

____

How did he make you feel?

____

____

____

Any red flags? YES or NO? If Yes, what was it?

____

____

____

____

____

____

DATING JOURNAL

Date:__________ Name of date:______________

Where were you?____________________________

What attracts you to him?

___

___

___

What stood out to you?

___

___

___

___

___

___

How did he make you feel?

___

___

___

Any red flags? YES or NO? If Yes, what was it?

___

___

___

___

___

___

DATING JOURNAL

Date:__________ Name of date:_______________

Where were you?_________________________________

What attracts you to him?

____

____

____

What stood out to you?

____

____

____

____

____

____

How did he make you feel?

____

____

____

Any red flags? YES or NO? If Yes, what was it?

____

____

____

____

____

____

DATING JOURNAL

Date:__________ Name of date:______________

Where were you?________________________________

What attracts you to him?

___

___

___

What stood out to you?

___

___

___

___

___

___

How did he make you feel?

___

___

___

Any red flags? YES or NO? If Yes, what was it?

___

___

___

___

___

___

DATING JOURNAL

Date:__________ Name of date:_______________

Where were you?_________________________________

What attracts you to him?

____

____

____

What stood out to you?

____

____

____

____

____

____

How did he make you feel?

____

____

____

Any red flags? YES or NO? If Yes, what was it?

____

____

____

____

____

____

DATING JOURNAL

Date:__________ Name of date:_______________

Where were you?______________________________________

What attracts you to him?

____

____

____

What stood out to you?

____

____

____

____

____

____

How did he make you feel?

____

____

____

Any red flags? YES or NO? If Yes, what was it?

____

____

____

____

____

____

DATING JOURNAL

Date:__________ Name of date:_______________

Where were you?____________________________________

What attracts you to him?

____

____

____

What stood out to you?

____

____

____

____

____

____

How did he make you feel?

____

____

____

Any red flags? YES or NO? If Yes, what was it?

____

____

____

____

____

____

DATING JOURNAL

Date:__________ Name of date:_______________

Where were you?_______________________________________

What attracts you to him?

____

____

____

What stood out to you?

____

____

____

____

____

____

How did he make you feel?

____

____

____

Any red flags? YES or NO? If Yes, what was it?

____

____

____

____

____

____

DATING JOURNAL

Date:__________ Name of date:_______________

Where were you?_________________________________

What attracts you to him?

____

____

____

What stood out to you?

____

____

____

____

____

____

How did he make you feel?

____

____

____

Any red flags? YES or NO? If Yes, what was it?

____

____

____

____

____

____

DATING JOURNAL

Date:__________ Name of date:_______________

Where were you?____________________________________

What attracts you to him?

What stood out to you?

How did he make you feel?

Any red flags? YES or NO? If Yes, what was it?

DATING JOURNAL

Date:__________ Name of date:_______________

Where were you?_________________________________

What attracts you to him?

What stood out to you?

How did he make you feel?

Any red flags? YES or NO? If Yes, what was it?

DATING JOURNAL

Date:__________ Name of date:______________

Where were you?____________________________________

What attracts you to him?

____

____

____

What stood out to you?

____

____

____

____

____

____

How did he make you feel?

____

____

____

Any red flags? YES or NO? If Yes, what was it?

____

____

____

____

____

____

DATING JOURNAL

Date:__________ Name of date:_______________

Where were you?________________________________

What attracts you to him?

____

____

____

What stood out to you?

____

____

____

____

____

____

How did he make you feel?

____

____

____

Any red flags? YES or NO? If Yes, what was it?

____

____

____

____

____

____

WHAT TO DO AFTER YOU THRIVE?

Your dating journal can help you decide if you want to keep the relationship or end it.

Staying in the relationship:

If you decide the relationship is worth pursuing further, awesome. Take comfort in knowing that you are now dating intentionally, and you have made steps to avoid having the wrong male experience.

Your dating journal however should not stop. Continue to keep track of your emotions, the behaviors and relationship dynamics.

Don't get so comfortable that you are not mindful. You may find after you decided to commit to the relationship that you are writing less, but be intentional about times that stand out, concerns you have and communicated needs.

Ending the relationship:

If you decided to end the relationship continue to the next page to complete the next discovery experience.

Go through this process with each person you date until you find the one that is made just for you.

Here you can write additional reflections. Are there additional thoughts, ideas, and challenges you must correct? Write it here:

ENDING THE RELATIONSHIP, BUT CONTINUING TO LEARN

Congratulations on sticking to your dating healthy plan. You are here because you have decided to end the relationship that you feel was not for you. It took a lot of courage and intentionality, but you did it. You avoided potential toxicity.

Regardless of who ended the relationship, it is important to learn from it. Take the time and truly explore what you have learned from that relationship and what you would do differently next time. Since you can only change yourself, it is important to keep the focus on you.

Now that the relationship has ended, review your journal entries. What have you noticed about yourself? What are some patterns of thinking that you recognize? Then complete the "Keeping track - Learning from your Relationships," page.

LEARNING FROM YOUR RELATIONSHIP

Date: __________ Relationship with: _________________________

What did you learn about yourself?

____

____

____

Are there areas of your life that you want to improve on? Why?

____

____

____

____

Is it reasonable? What will it take? How will you start?

____

____

____

KEEPING TRACK

Learning from your relationships.

Date: __________ Relationship with: __________________________

What did you learn about yourself?

____

____

____

Are there areas of your life that you want to improve on? Why?

____

____

____

____

Is it reasonable? What will it take? How will you start?

____

____

____

KEEPING TRACK

Learning from your relationships.

Date: __________ Relationship with: ______________________________

What did you learn about yourself?

____

____

____

Are there areas of your life that you want to improve on? Why?

____

____

____

____

Is it reasonable? What will it take? How will you start?

____

____

____

KEEPING TRACK

Learning from your relationships.

Date: __________ Relationship with: __________________________

What did you learn about yourself?

____

____

____

Are there areas of your life that you want to improve on? Why?

____

____

____

____

Is it reasonable? What will it take? How will you start?

____

____

____

KEEPING TRACK

Learning from your relationships.

Date: __________ Relationship with: ________________________

What did you learn about yourself?

____

____

____

Are there areas of your life that you want to improve on? Why?

____

____

____

____

Is it reasonable? What will it take? How will you start?

____

____

____

KEEPING TRACK

Learning from your relationships.

Date: _________ Relationship with: _______________________

What did you learn about yourself?

____

____

____

Are there areas of your life that you want to improve on? Why?

____

____

____

____

Is it reasonable? What will it take? How will you start?

____

____

____

KEEPING TRACK

Learning from your relationships.

Date: __________ Relationship with: __________________________

What did you learn about yourself?

____

____

____

Are there areas of your life that you want to improve on? Why?

____

____

____

____

Is it reasonable? What will it take? How will you start?

____

____

____

KEEPING TRACK

Learning from your relationships.

Date: __________ Relationship with: __________________________

What did you learn about yourself?

____

____

____

Are there areas of your life that you want to improve on? Why?

____

____

____

____

Is it reasonable? What will it take? How will you start?

____

____

____

KEEPING TRACK

Learning from your relationships.

Date: __________ Relationship with: ________________________

What did you learn about yourself?

____

____

____

Are there areas of your life that you want to improve on? Why?

____

____

____

____

Is it reasonable? What will it take? How will you start?

____

____

____

KEEPING TRACK

Learning from your relationships.

Date: __________ Relationship with: __________________________

What did you learn about yourself?

____

____

____

Are there areas of your life that you want to improve on? Why?

____

____

____

____

Is it reasonable? What will it take? How will you start?

____

____

____

GOING BACK

You're Just Not Ready

Everyone's journey is different and sometimes, we go back. Going back is your individual decision, but it should be made with awareness.

There are a few reasons women continue to stay in unhealthy relationships.

Often women go back because of promises that it is going to be different this time and it may. Even when going back, do so intentionally. What exactly is going to be different? Is the difference something you can measure and see? Is the difference something he actually communicated?

If this is you, write out what you expect to happen and periodically check to see if it is happening. Include your observations in your dating journal along the way.

What are the promises being made? What do you expect to be different?

Date:______________

Promise/Expectation:_____________________________________

____

Healing Is Power!

Date:_______________

Promise/Expectation:____

____

Date:_______________

Promise/Expectation:____

____

Date:_______________

Promise/Expectation:____

____

Date:_______________

Promise/Expectation:____

____

Date:_______________

Promise/Expectation:____

____

Healing Is Power!

Date:______________

Promise/Expectation:____________________________________

____

Date:______________

Promise/Expectation:____________________________________

____

Date:______________

Promise/Expectation:____________________________________

____

Date:______________

Promise/Expectation:____________________________________

____

Date:______________

Promise/Expectation:____________________________________

____

For a Purpose

Other times, women go back because there is an unmet need that they feel holds them there, perhaps because of financial reasons, nowhere to go, afraid to leave, concerns about children, etc.

If you want to leave the relationship, but just don't feel ready yet, be intentional about developing a plan.

What is your reason(s) for staying?

____

____

____

What needs to happen before you can leave?

____

____

____

What steps will you take to get there?

____

____

____

What is your time frame?

____

Stay mindful of your reason for staying in the unhealthy relationship and develop your plan.

If you want to leave the relationship, but just don't feel ready yet, be intentional about developing a plan.

What is your reason(s) for staying?

____

____

____

____

What needs to happen before you can leave?

____

____

____

____

____

What steps will you take to get there?

____

____

____

What is your time frame?

____

Stay mindful of your reason for staying in the unhealthy relationship and develop your plan.

If you want to leave the relationship, but just don't feel ready yet, be intentional about developing a plan.

What is your reason(s) for staying?

____

____

____

____

What needs to happen before you can leave?

____

____

____

____

____

What steps will you take to get there?

____

____

____

What is your time frame?

____

Stay mindful of your reason for staying in the unhealthy relationship and develop your plan.

If you want to leave the relationship, but just don't feel ready yet, be intentional about developing a plan.

What is/are your reason(s) for staying?

____

____

____

____

What needs to happen before you can leave?

____

____

____

____

____

What steps will you take to get there?

____

____

____

What is your time frame?

____

Stay mindful of your reason for staying in the unhealthy relationship and develop your plan.

If you want to leave the relationship, but just don't feel ready yet, be intentional about developing a plan.

What is/are your reason(s) for staying?

____

____

____

____

What needs to happen before you can leave?

____

____

____

____

____

What steps will you take to get there?

____

____

____

What is your time frame?

____

Extras

Positive Traits and Characteristics List

Accepting
Brave
Confident
Creative
Down-to-Earth
Focused
Frugal
Goofy
Helpful
Independent
Intelligent
Loyal
Motivated
Optimistic
Attractive
Cheerful
Cooperative
Decisive
Enthusiastic
Modest

Forgiving
Funny
Grateful
Honest
Innovative
Kind
Mature
Nurturing
Organized
Balanced
Courteous
Determined
Flexible
Friendly
Generous
Hardworking
Humble
Insightful
Listener
Open-Minded

Respectful
Selfless
Skilled
Tolerant
Sensitive
Smart
Trusting
Thoughtful
Strong
Responsible
Serious
Reliable
Relaxed
Positive
Self-Directed
Practical
Resilient
Patient
Realistic
Financially secure

JOURNAL SAMPLES

Rethinking how you see dating and boundaries can be difficult. To help navigate this process, included are samples to serve as a guideline for how to complete your, "Dating Journal," as well as, "Ending the Relationship, but Continuing to Learn," process.

Dating Journal

SAMPLE - Dating Journal

Name: Jon Date: Feb 9

Where were you? He came to visit me.

What attracts you to him?
I met him while he was in town on business. We exchanged numbers and talked for hours about everything. On this day he came to visit me after talking every day for hours for 2 weeks. He flew down to see me!

What stood out to you?
He initially said he was structured and afraid of committing but later that evening he states he is ready to be exclusive. I asked, and he agreed to hold off on commitment until I have had time to visit him. I wanted to see how he was living before committing, make sure there was no wife at home...
Since I tend to love freely, I viewed it as having some influence on him. I felt somewhat empowered and happy to have influenced this freedom to love.

How did he make you feel?
He made me feel valued, we held so much in common. Our views on church, politics and community issues were the same. we laughed a lot. He was patient and went with the flow. I like that - I didn't feel rushed or pressured to spend every moment with him. He was independent and found things to do when I was not available. I appreciated that.

Any red flags? Yes or (No) If yes, what was it? No

SAMPLE - Dating Journal

Name: Jon Date: Mar 1

Where were you? He came to visit again!

What attracts you to him? He continues to be attentive and consistent.

What stood out to you?
He continues to be attentive and have a desire to satisfy me. He speaks openly about his feelings for me. He opens doors and takes me out. He continues to get a hotel when he comes with no pressure.

How did he make you feel? Feeling cared for, as if we could do whatever I wanted. I feel really good about him. He seems to be a great guy! I shared some secrets with him and he responded well.

Red flags/concerns: He does not have children, I don't want children.

SAMPLE - Dating Journal

Name: Jon   Date: March 21

Where were you? Talking over the phone.

What attracts you to him? His conversation. We can talk about a variety of topics and we find agreeance, sharing similar views.

What stood out to you?
Our relationship is still going great! We talk a lot about traveling together and meeting each other's family and friends.
He wants me to go visit but due to my schedule it has been impossible he does seem a little annoyed with that and is sticking with no commitment until I visit him despite me now wanting the commitment.

How did he make you feel?
I'm still feeling very good about the relationship since our communication is consistent.
Feeling a little confused by why he initially wanted the commitment but now is stuck on me visiting first. I always say, God is not a God of confusion, where there is confusion God is not present... Still hoping for the best but mindful.

Any red flags? (Yes) or No If yes, what was it?
Nothing just yet, but I am aware that there is some inconsistency.

SAMPLE - Dating Journal

Name: Jon Date: April 8

When and where were you? Phone conversation.

What attracts you to him? His continued interest in me. We continue to have great conversation.

What stood out to you?

I said I was going to tentatively visit… why did I say that?

My son's plan for the weekend fell through and I couldn't go. Around the same time, his job task changed.

How did he make you feel?

I feel bad that he was disappointed/hurt (his words) that I was not able to go but says he understands.

Feeling some level of responsibility, a feeling of obligation to make it right.

Any red flags? (Yes) or No If yes, what was it?

He says he understands but seems annoyed. I guess I understand but I don't like the way it makes me feel.

SAMPLE - Dating Journal

Name: Jon Date: May 12

Where were you? We met in a mutual city.

What attracts you to him?
His display of disappointment of not seeing me. His availability, although he is calling less, he always answers when I call him.

What stood out to you?
When I first saw him, he seemed aloof... no excitement... it was like... oh hey...
But I was too excited I brushed it off and showed my excitement. He adjusted and smiled... then became more like the guy I initially met, the guy that wanted the immediate commitment. He showed that he was happy to see me and said it.

How did he make you feel?
I had a mix of emotions this weekend. I initially felt special, he was willing to take the road trip for me. I know he did it for me and I appreciated the sacrifice. Although there were some moments of awkwardness, we ended our time well. On my drive home I started to replay our interactions. I am being intentional

Any red flags? (Yes) or No If yes, what was it?
Yes, He never did say what he wanted even though I asked. I know that if he wanted more he would say more. I am questioning if I want more from him...

Learning from your Relationship

Journal Sample

Date: June 1 Relationship with: Jon

What did you learn about yourself:

In this relationship, there were good times, but I recognized that I was starting to get annoyed by his lack of calling back and keeping his word. I remind myself - I am worth someone being consistent with and honest, if Jon cannot do that, he cannot occupy my space. While I did express my disappointment when times came up, he was always apologetic and asked what he could to make it better. He would fix it for a while but eventually return to being inconsistent.

Are there areas of your life that you want to improve on? Why?

I will continue to work on not getting caught in the "Why trap". While I want to know why, I accept that I will not know why someone will say they love me and turn around and do things that he knows would at a minimum annoy me. I am not doing that. I accept him how he is and choose to remove myself.

I will also not share my secrets so easy, I realize I wanted it to work more because of that.

Is it reasonable? What will it take? How will you start?

Yes, I will implement immediately.

GET CONNECTED

Wow! You took this step to gain your personal healing, how Awesome is that?!? You should feel very proud of yourself.

I know however that healing can sometimes be even harder than you thought and even though you have completed the steps there are times that things are still hard. Please know, that it is totally normal. As suggested in the beginning of the book, therapy in conjunction with this book can be very beneficial. I have also created a few other platforms to ensure you don't have to go on your healing journey alone.

Join me and other women just like you!

Facebook group - Heal, Date, Thrive! – a private membership group of women who have the book and are going through the same steps. The group will serve as peer support, but I will also share regular motivational post, go live weekly and will answer individual questions. You already have your book, connect today!

Heal. Date. Thrive. Circle: Create your own tribe of women and I will come to you and facilitate a step by step discussion! The HDT Circle connects your friends and family members together with the purpose of getting your tribe on the same path of healing and dating healthy. This connection is designed to help provide a consistent network of support and accountability. For additional details visit us online: www.healingispower.net

Healing Is Power!

The Power Circle

The Power Circle is a movement of normalizing healing. Joining the movement explores additional ways to achieve true and long-lasting healing. This healing is not just relationship healing, we seek to create an overall sense of internal peace in all areas of life. Why not heal while having fun? The Power Circle explores everything from interviews and educational podcast to music and DIYs.

Follow Lakisha:

www.healingispower.net

"It is difficult to heal in isolation, get connected!"

About the Author

Lakisha M Harris, MA, LPC

~~With over twenty years of experience working with youth, parents, and families, Lakisha seeks to enhance the world one family at a time. Lakisha has demonstrated knowledge and expertise of the needs of women of all ages. She is passionate about the impacts that true healing provides and coined the statement, "Healing Is Power!" In all her work, she seeks to normalize the healing process in order to develop an atmosphere of true happy living.

Lakisha has an understanding and empathy for life's challenges and know how to best support individuals through the process. Her personable demeanor and genuine care for the well-being of those she works with, naturally draws people in. She specializes in supporting individuals and families seeking to enhance their current life situation and assist with putting the pieces of life together.

Lakisha earned her BS in Criminal Justice from UNC-Charlotte and MA in Professional Counseling from Liberty University. She is a Licensed Professional Counselor in NC specializing in childhood trauma and women's issues and is an Accredited Parent coach.

Acknowledgements

I acknowledge that becoming who I am today, my passion, my determination and commitment has been a journey. One that I appreciate and embrace. I have had relationships that have taught me so many things, both positive lessons to live by and negative lessons to avoid. Throughout it all, I have been blessed to be surrounded by people who love me and allow me to be me, (as if they had a choice, LOL).

Those very special family members are: My children ***Caylah and Jadah Harris*** *– my truest loves and greatest accomplishments. They serve as my daily motivation to create a world of happiness, healing, and wholeness.* ***Linda Gill,*** *(my mother, who instilled the belief that I can truly be anything I wanted and supports everything her children do)!* ***Malika Harris,*** *(my twin sister who has been my day-one, my sounding board, and financial thinker).* ***Conan Harris,*** *(my brother, who has been the reminder that my motivation and encouragement make a difference. He embodies perseverance)!* ***Ieasha James,*** *(my little sister/Event Planner Extraordinaire of Endless Flair Events, who has been one of my greatest supporters of this book, my motivation to finish it and a true believer of the power of healing)!* ***Ayanna Pressley,*** *(my sister in law and Congresswoman who exemplifies the belief of being unapologetically you)!* ***My dad, little sister, step-daughter, aunts, uncles and numerous cousins*** *who believed God desired to use me and so He did.*

To my many friends, (way too many to name), who have stepped in to encourage, love on and support me. To my branding coach ***Elyshia Brooks*** *who God saw fit to make this connection and help build my brand.* ***To my clients*** *who had enough belief in me to allow me to guide them on their journey of healing. And to each of you who have picked up this book...*

Thank you!

Made in the USA
Coppell, TX
23 November 2022